THE STORY OF HOPE

Discovering the Provision in God's Plan

Good Soil
Evangelism & Discipleship

The Story of Hope: Discovering the Provision in God's Plan

Fourth Edition, February 2011
Copyright 2007-2011 by
Good Soil Evangelism and Discipleship

Association of Baptists for World Evangelism
P.O. Box 8585
Harrisburg, PA 17105 USA
Phone: (877) 959-2293

980 Adelaide Street South, Suite 34
London, Ontario N6E 1R3 CANADA
Phone: (877) 690-1009

Cover & Story Art: Justinen Creative Group

Layout Design: Mike Fields

Authors: Wayne Haston & Ron Berrus

  Haston, Wayne 1947-
  Berrus, Ron 1954-

ISBN 1-888796-37-5 (Trade Paper)

Library of Congress Cataloging-in-Publications Data (application pending)

All Scripture quotations are taken from the New King James Version® (NKJV®) of the Bible (Thomas Nelson, Inc.).

Printed in the United States of America.

Email: Info@GoodSoil.com
Web: www.GoodSoil.com

CONTENTS

INTRODUCTION

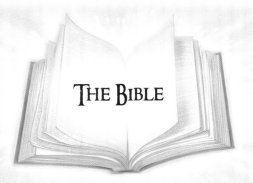

THE BIBLE

The Bible is the most amazing book ever written. Imagine this: The 66 books of the Bible were written over a period of more than 1,500 years by approximately 40 different authors who represent a wide range of historical eras, geographical settings, political and cultural perspectives, levels of literacy, occupations, family backgrounds, and human personalities. Various parts of the Bible were written in three different languages on three continents.

This remarkable book contains more than 500 stories involving nearly 3,000 characters. Yet beautifully interwoven from cover to cover through all of the Bible's various stories is one Big Story. It's a story that has an attention-grabbing opening, a clear and intriguing plot, a strong and interesting central character, many diverse and colorful supporting characters, numerous mysteries that are unveiled along the way, and a dramatically climactic ending. It's a story that begins wonderfully, then goes terribly wrong, and ultimately ends better than most readers would have imagined. And on top of all that, it's a TRUE story.

The Bible is worthy of reading and study, even if you are skeptical about what you think you know about its message. This enduring piece of world literature is consistently ranked as a bestseller in many regions and countries of the world. One who has not read the Bible in its entirety can hardly consider himself or herself to be broadly and deeply educated.

People well-acquainted with the Bible and its Big Story do not marvel at the book's popularity. They understand the reason readers become deeply attracted to it when they begin to study its Big Story with open minds. It's all about the timeless and universal need that this story addresses and the satisfactory provision for that need that it offers. It's truly *The Story of Hope*—the story that unveils God's unique provision in His plan to bring eternal hope to people of all times and places.

As is true with any classic work of literature, the Bible can best be understood and appreciated if it is studied seriously from beginning to end. This Bible study book will help you to do just that.

INSTRUCTIONS

Tips for Self-Study

- Start at the storyline's beginning on page 12 and continue systematically to the end on page 31. Then study The Chronological Bridge to Life on pages 32-39, which summarizes eight essential truths that emerge out of the Bible's Big Story.

- Often it will be helpful for you to refer to the Bible maps on pages 7-9 and the tabernacle visual on page 10. The maps will give you a good visual sense of the story's setting, and the tabernacle visual will help you to understand how God-seekers in the early part of the Bible found hope.

- Read the study questions and Bible passages for each event and follow the study instructions. These questions have been designed to help you digest the Big Story of this big book, the Bible, in a relatively short amount of time.

- If you have questions, do not let those stop you. Some of your questions will be answered as you continue through the study. Just let the story speak for itself. If you still have questions after you have completed the study, seek answers from someone who knows the Bible well or contact Info@GoodSoil.com.

- Think of the Bible's Big Story as a mystery story. Look for clues that gradually unveil the plot and enjoy the experience of seeing the plot tensions resolved and the story emerge progressively into clear understanding.

- You will find some additional self-study tips in the section below, even though that material is primarily focused on leader-guided studies.

- If you would be willing to share your experiences as a participant in this study, please do so at www.GoodSoil.com.

Suggestions for Group Study Leaders

Although *The Story of Hope* can be self-studied, it is generally even more effective in leader-guided Bible studies, with one participant or a small group of learners.

- During the study sessions, read aloud the Bible study questions and Bible passages. It will be helpful to share these reading opportunities with all members of the study group. Make it a truly participative study and keep each participant actively engaged in personal study of the Biblical texts.

- To speed up the study, develop a way in which participants can locate the Bible passages quickly. Some options:
  (1) Prepare a printed handout containing the texts of all of the passages.
  (2) Give each participant a copy of the same edition of the Bible so that you can use page numbers to help them locate Bible passages.
  (3) In those Bibles mark the verses that will be used during the study.

- Realize that *The Story of Hope* is designed to allow for several different levels of Bible study, each involving a different degree of time commitment. Some options:

- **The 15 to 60 minutes scenario:** Beginning with page 12 and continuing through page 31, point to each event image and read the summary statements associated with each of the 40 Bible events or summarize the event in your own words. If

Suggestions for Group Study Leaders *(Continued)*

the participant expresses interest in the story, briefly explain how The Chronological Bridge to Life relates to the Bible's Big Story and summarize each of the eight essential "bridge truths" on pages 32-39. Give the participant a copy of *The Story of Hope* and your contact information.

- **The 2 to 6 hours scenario:** Go through the entire storyline as well as The Chronological Bridge to Life, but only read and explain a few of the Bible passages that are most important to explaining the Big Story.

- **The 14 or more hours scenario:** Use the discussion questions associated with each Bible event, read each referenced Bible passage, and elaborate and interact as necessary to help the participant fully understand the Big Story.

- **Hybrid options:** Use some combination of the above options, perhaps focusing more on events, passages, and questions that are most pertinent to the core redemptive message of the story.

- **Pre-session study:** If there is sufficient commitment on the part of the Bible study participants, make Bible study assignments in advance of upcoming study sessions. This will help to minimize the amount of reading to be done during the session and will allow for quicker and more thoughtful responses to discussion questions.

- The study questions will surface several recurring themes at various points throughout the study. Be aware of these themes and emphasize them as you lead the study: God's provision of paradise, the offspring of the woman who will conquer Satan, the significance of the lamb and the shedding of its blood as the means for the forgiveness of sins, God's promise to bless all families of the earth through Abraham, conscious eternal punishment for Satan and unbelievers, and a King from Judah who will reign forever.

- Take full advantage of the Bible maps on pages 7-9 at every appropriate point. Also, it is very important that you use the tabernacle visual on page 10 at the appropriate time in order to clearly explain the features and functions of the tabernacle. Place special emphasis on what happens at the altar near the entry way of the tabernacle court, as described in Leviticus 1.

- Always use the information at the bottom of each double-page spread to help the participant focus on what he or she learned on those two pages about God (in the Old Testament section) and Jesus Christ (in the New Testament section). Teach, emphasize, and constantly reinforce the fact that as we read through the Bible, we progressively learn more and more about God and His Son, Jesus Christ.

- Avoid controversial topics that are not essential to the redemptive story and guide the focus to remain on God, Jesus, and the overall Big Story. If these types of controversial issues arise, ask participants to record their questions and bring them up again after you have completed studying *The Story of Hope*.

- Avoid the temptation to unveil answers to the story's mysteries before the story unveils them. Let the story unfold chronologically and avoid explaining what Old Testament events are foreshadowing prior to their fulfillments. Very important!

- Upon the completion of your study of *The Story of Hope*, use *The Hope* DVD to summarize and review what your group has studied. That DVD is available through www.thehopeproject.com.

- Download the free Leader's Guide for *The Story of Hope* from the user support site and learn of other related resources. Also, please submit feedback regarding your experiences using *The Story of Hope*.

User Support Site: www.GoodSoil.com

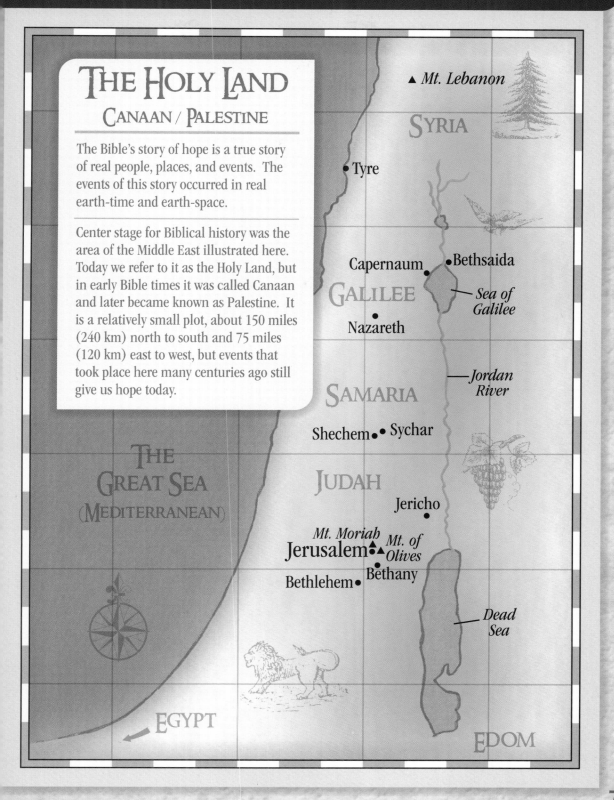

THE HOLY LAND
CANAAN / PALESTINE

The Bible's story of hope is a true story of real people, places, and events. The events of this story occurred in real earth-time and earth-space.

Center stage for Biblical history was the area of the Middle East illustrated here. Today we refer to it as the Holy Land, but in early Bible times it was called Canaan and later became known as Palestine. It is a relatively small plot, about 150 miles (240 km) north to south and 75 miles (120 km) east to west, but events that took place here many centuries ago still give us hope today.

▲ Mt. Lebanon

SYRIA

• Tyre

Capernaum • Bethsaida

GALILEE

Sea of Galilee

Nazareth

Jordan River

SAMARIA

Shechem • Sychar

THE GREAT SEA (MEDITERRANEAN)

JUDAH

Jericho

Mt. Moriah Mt. of Olives
Jerusalem ▲▲

Bethany

Bethlehem •

Dead Sea

EGYPT

EDOM

MAP OF THE ANCIENT NEAR EAST

Just as the Holy Land, illustrated on page 7, was center stage for the most important events in *The Story of Hope*, this broader region was the extended platform where many other Bible events occurred. Historians call it the Ancient Near East, but today we know of it as the Middle East. The area from Canaan to Chaldea in the green zone of the map has also been called the Fertile Crescent, because of the arable land there.

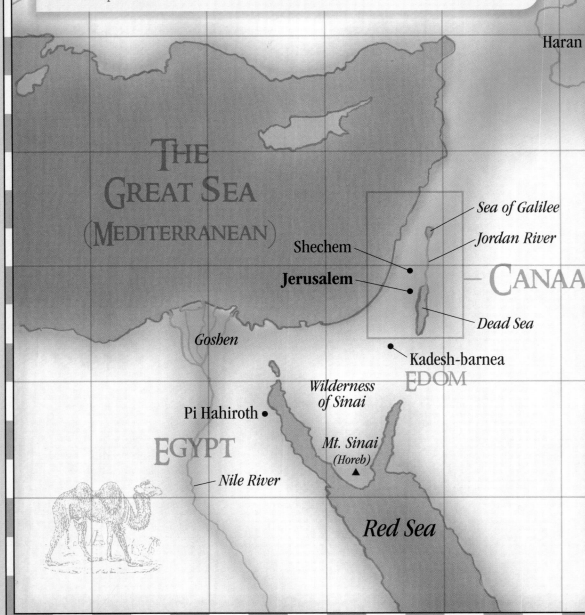

Haran

THE GREAT SEA (MEDITERRANEAN)

Sea of Galilee

Jordan River

Shechem

Jerusalem

CANAA

Dead Sea

Goshen

Kadesh-barnea

EDOM

Wilderness of Sinai

Pi Hahiroth •

EGYPT

Mt. Sinai (Horeb) ▲

Nile River

Red Sea

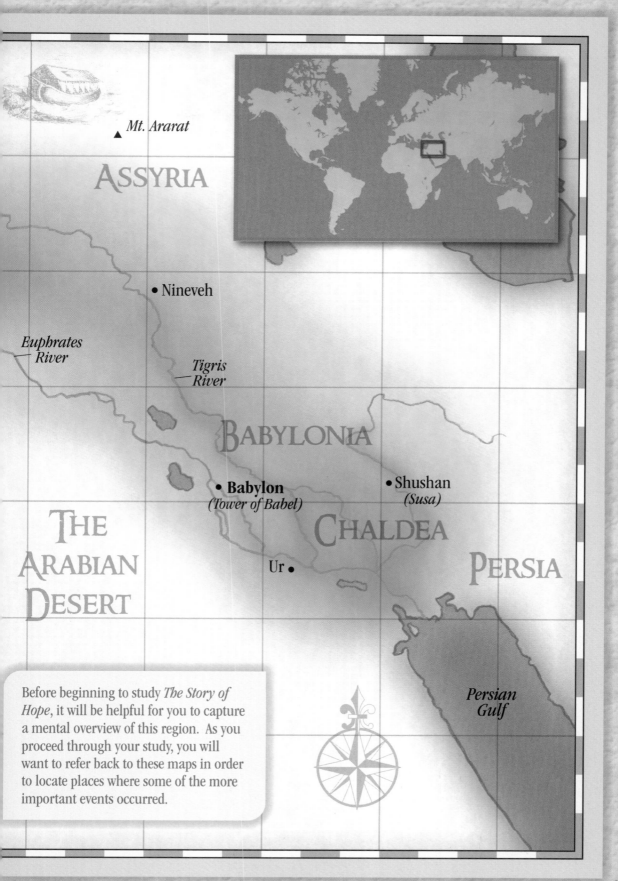

Mt. Ararat

ASSYRIA

• Nineveh

Euphrates
River

Tigris
River

BABYLONIA

• **Babylon**
(Tower of Babel)

• Shushan
(Susa)

THE
ARABIAN
DESERT

CHALDEA

PERSIA

Ur •

Persian
Gulf

Before beginning to study *The Story of Hope*, it will be helpful for you to capture a mental overview of this region. As you proceed through your study, you will want to refer back to these maps in order to locate places where some of the more important events occurred.

THE TABERNACLE

This curious-looking structure plays an important role in the first half of *The Story of Hope*.

Later in the study, you will be directed to return to this visual to learn why and how this mobile tabernacle became a symbol of hope and promise for many God-seekers who lived a long time ago.

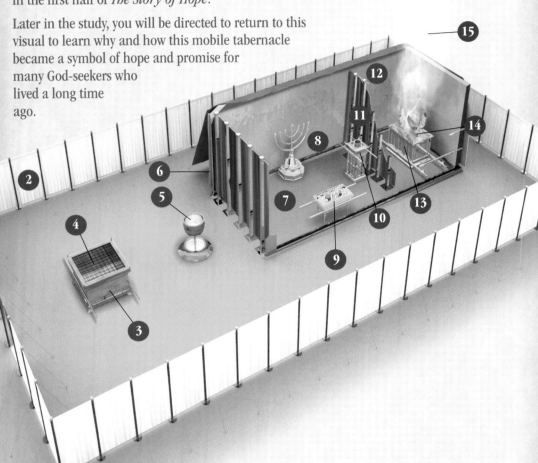

(artwork not to scale)

Features

1. Gate of the Court
2. Court Fence
3. Bronze Altar
4. Offerings at the Altar
5. Bronze Laver (Basin)
6. Tabernacle
7. Holy Place
8. Golden Lampstand
9. Table of Bread
10. Altar of Incense
11. Veil
12. Most Holy Place
13. Ark of the Covenant
14. Mercy Seat
15. Pillar of Fire & Cloud

THE STORY OF HOPE

On the following page, you will begin the fascinating study of God's masterplan for the universe, the spirit world, and the human race. You will learn the answer to some of the great questions common to men and women of all times and places: How did I get here? What is the meaning of life? How can I realize that meaning in my life? What lies beyond the grave? How can I be prepared to die?

Turn the page and begin your experience with the true, unfolding drama of *The Story of Hope*.

1

In its opening statement, the Bible addresses the most basic issue of human existence by declaring that the something or someone who has always existed is God.

In the beginning God...

The Eternal God

Genesis 1:1

a. Why is it reasonable to assume that *something* or *someone* has always existed?

b. Read the first phrase of Genesis 1:1. Which of the following is true? Explain the reasoning behind your choice.
☐ *The Bible begins with an attempt to prove the existence of God.*
☐ *The Bible begins with the assumption that God exists.*

c. Read Psalm 90:2. What does it mean that God is "from everlasting to everlasting"?

d. As we read through the Bible, we learn more and more about God—who He is and what He is like. At the bottom of each double-page spread (such as this one, pages 12-13) place a mark beside each of the ways God is portrayed in the four events on the two pages.

e. The Hebrew word for God used here is "Elohim," which means the "Strong One."

2

The Bible continues by saying that God created the universe including our earth and its heavens, as well as its living organisms—plants and animals of all kinds.

Creation of the Earth

Genesis 1:1-25

a. First day of creation—Read verses 1-5.
• In its initial state of creation (verse 2), what was the earth like?
• What did God do in verses 3-5?

b. Second day of creation—Read verses 6-8. What did God divide on this day?

c. Third day of creation—Read verses 9-13.
• What happened first on the third day? (verses 9-10)
• What happened next on this same day? (verses 11-13)

d. Fourth day of creation—Read verses 14-19. What were some of God's earth-related purposes for the lights in the earth's heavens?

e. Fifth day of creation—Read verses 20-23. What animals were created on this day?

f. Sixth day of creation, part 1—Read verses 24-25. What animals were created next?

Put a mark beside each of the ways that Go

☐ Almighty Creator   ☐ Supreme Authority   ☐ Just Judge   ☐ Merciful Protecto
☐ Holy God   ☐ Faithful Promise Keeper   ☐ Eternal Bein

3 Then God created a man and a woman, Adam and Eve, and commissioned them to rule over His earthly creation, but told them not to eat the fruit of one particular tree.

Creation of Mankind

Genesis 1:26-31; Genesis 2:7-25

a. Read Genesis 1:26-27. Compared to the other creatures God made, what was unique and special about the creation of man and woman?

b. Read Genesis 1:28-31. What special role did God give to them that was not given to other creatures that God made?

c. Read Genesis 2:7. What additional facts do we learn here regarding the creation of Adam?

d. Read Genesis 2:8-9. What indications do we see in these verses that the Garden of Eden was a beautiful and fruitful paradise?

e. Read Genesis 2:15-17. What one thing did God tell Adam not to do and what did God say would happen if this command was disobeyed?

f. Read Genesis 2:18-25. True or False? *At this time, Adam and Eve were living in a condition of innocence.* What do you see in these verses that leads to your conclusion?

4 At some earlier time Lucifer, originally a beautiful angel of God, led other angels in a failed rebellion against God and became known as Satan, the Devil.

Fall of Lucifer

Ezekiel 28:11-17; Isaiah 14:12-15

a. Angels are spirit beings that God created to worship and serve Him.

b. Many Bible teachers believe that Ezekiel and Isaiah provided a description of Lucifer's downfall by comparing Lucifer to the kings of Tyre and Babylon.
   • Read Ezekiel 28:11-17. What was Lucifer originally like?
   • Read Isaiah 14:12-15. What did Lucifer aspire to do that led to his downfall? In verse 15, what did God say would happen to him?

c. Read Matthew 25:41. How does this verse relate to Isaiah 14:15? Hint: The "Devil" is another name for Lucifer.

d. Who do you think the Devil's angels are—the ones mentioned in Matthew 25:41?

e. We do not know exactly when Lucifer rebelled. It may have been much earlier, but it certainly occurred before the following event.

portrayed in the events on these pages:

Universally Present Spirit ☐ All-Knowing One ☐ Relational Person ☐ Loving Father
Authoritative Lawgiver ☐ Forgiving Redeemer ☐ Truth Revealer

5 In continued defiance against God, Satan enticed Eve to eat of the forbidden tree and Eve then influenced Adam to do the same, in spite of God's clear and loving warning.

Beginning of Human Sin

Genesis 3:1-6

a. Keep in mind this phrase from the last book of the Bible: "The dragon, that serpent of old, who is the Devil and Satan." (Revelation 20:2)

b. Read Genesis 3:1-5. Satan appeared to Eve in the form of a serpent and...

☐ Misquoted God to make Him seem to be unloving (compare Genesis 2:16-17 with 3:1).

☐ Denied that God could or would punish disobedience as He had promised (see verse 4).

☐ Suggested that God only gave this warning because He is selfish and jealous (see verse 5).

c. True or false? *Satan wanted Eve to doubt that God is good, true to His promises, and holy.*

d. Read Genesis 3:6. What three factors motivated Eve to eat the fruit that God had forbidden?

e. As we study the Bible, it is important to realize that any act of disobedience against what God has commanded is called *sin*.

6 Because God is a holy and just judge, Adam and Eve suffered the consequences of their disobedience; they immediately died spiritually and eventually died physically.

Origin of Death

Genesis 3:7-13; Genesis 5:5

a. The essence of death is separation. Three kinds of death result from sin: spiritual death, physical death, and an eternal death.

b. Read Genesis 3:7-13. What indications do you see here that Adam and Eve's sin resulted in the following:

☐ Spiritual death (separation from God), which caused a...

☐ Deep sense of guilt, shame, and fear, which led to...

☐ Problems in their relationship with each other.

c. Read Genesis 5:5. What other penalty did Adam eventually have to experience for his sin?

d. Read Genesis 5:8, 11, 14, 17, 20, 27, and 31. Then, read Romans 5:12. In what two ways are we all affected by Adam's disobedience in Genesis 3?

7 God then promised that a special offspring of Eve would someday conquer Satan because of Satan's evil participation in Adam and Eve's disobedience.

Promise of a Satan Conqueror

Genesis 3:14-15

a. Read Genesis 3:14. What changes did God impose upon the serpent-animal?

b. Read Genesis 3:15. Choose one interpretation:
   ☐ God was simply establishing hostility between people and snakes.
   ☐ No, something more significant was happening here.

c. The "seed" (offspring) of the woman would: (check all that are true)
   ☐ Be a male human being.
   ☐ Damage one of the most significant parts of the serpent's body.
   ☐ Suffer harm to a less significant part of his body in the process of defeating the serpent.

d. Keep this in mind: This person would be the seed (offspring) of the woman—no mention was made that he would be the seed or offspring of man!

8 After Adam and Eve attempted to cover their guilt and shame with fig leaves, God graciously replaced the leaves with clothing He made from animal skins.

Provision of Coverings

Genesis 3:7, 21

a. Read Genesis 3:7 and then read Genesis 3:21.

b. Look for at least two differences between the manner in which Adam and Eve were clothed in verse 7 and the way they were clothed in verse 21. Hints: Who prepared the coverings? What kinds of coverings were used?

c. True or False? *Based upon what we know that God did for them, it seems that Adam and Eve's loss of innocence was permanent.*

d. True or False? *It appears that Adam and Eve's sin made it necessary for one or more innocent animals to be killed to provide these coverings.*

portrayed in the events on these pages:

☐ Universally Present Spirit   ☐ All-Knowing One   ☐ Relational Person   ☐ Loving Father
☐ Authoritative Lawgiver   ☐ Forgiving Redeemer   ☐ Truth Revealer

9 Because Adam and Eve's disobedience caused them to forfeit their privilege to live in the paradise garden where God had placed them, God drove them out of it.

Banishment from Eden

Genesis 3:22-24

a. Read the first statement in Genesis 3:22. True or False? *Because they had eaten fruit from the forbidden tree, Adam and Eve now had knowledge of evil from personal experience.* If so, how is this different from God's knowledge of evil?

b. Read the second half of verse 22 in Genesis 3 and on through 3:24.
   • Fact 1: Verses 23-24 tell us that God expelled Adam and Eve from the Garden of Eden.
   • Fact 2: The second part of verse 22 reveals God's reason for expelling them.

c. Questions regarding the banishment of Adam and Eve from the Garden of Eden:
   • Was this an act of God's judgment? Explain.
   • Was this also in some way a gracious act of God? Explain.

10 Throughout the years to follow, the human race grew and became so sinful that God destroyed the earth and its inhabitants with a great flood, except for God-fearing Noah and his family.

The Great Flood

Genesis 6:5—8:22

a. Read Genesis 6:5-7, 11-12. What influenced God to send such a devastating flood? How serious was this problem that caused the flood?

b. Read Genesis 6:8-10 and 7:1. How did Noah differ from the other people of his generation? What do you think it meant that "Noah walked with God"?

c. Read Genesis 6:5—8:22. If we take this story at face value (literally), does it appear that this flood was:

☐ A local flood?
☐ A worldwide flood?

d. Read Genesis 6:15. How large was the ark?

e. From this story, what do we learn about:
   • Mankind?
   • God?

Put a mark beside each of the ways that Go

☐ Almighty Creator   ☐ Supreme Authority   ☐ Just Judge   ☐ Merciful Protect
☐ Holy God   ☐ Faithful Promise Keeper   ☐ Eternal Bein

11 Many years after the flood, God called Abraham to be the father of a very large nation through whom all peoples of the earth would receive a special spiritual blessing.

Promises to Abraham

Genesis 11:31—12:7

a. Read Genesis 11:31-32 and locate Ur, Haran, and Canaan on the map on pages 8 and 9.

b. Read Genesis 12:1-3. At the end of verse 3 there is one special promise to keep in mind. Since the promise that all families of the earth would be blessed through Abraham is repeated several times in the Bible, obviously it is very important. In what sense could this promise be realized? To learn the answer to this question, you will need to wait and see how the Bible's story of hope eventually develops.

c. Read Genesis 12:4-7. What additional promise did God give Abraham in verse 7?

12 God tested Abraham's faith by asking him to sacrifice Isaac, his son through whom the spiritual blessing would come, but at the last moment God provided a substitute sacrifice.

Offering of Isaac

Genesis 22:1-18

a. Read Genesis 22:1-14. Why do you think...
   • God asked Abraham to sacrifice his son?
   • Abraham obeyed this unusual command?

b. The answers are related to what Abraham believed that God could and would do for him.
   • Re-read verse 5. Then read Hebrews 11:17-19. What did Abraham believe that God could do?
   • Re-read Genesis 22:7-14.
   How was Abraham's faith confirmed in this case?

c. Read Genesis 22:15-18. What promise do you see in verse 18? What is slightly different here, as compared to Genesis 12:3? Hint: Compare "in you..." with "in your seed (offspring)...."

d. Later, Isaac had a son named Jacob (whom God renamed *Israel*) who had twelve sons. As Israel was preparing to die, what promise did he make to his son Judah in the first few words of Genesis 49:10? Hint: A scepter is a staff held by a king as a symbol of royal authority.

portrayed in the events on these pages:

Universally Present Spirit   ☐ All-Knowing One   ☐ Relational Person   ☐ Loving Father
Authoritative Lawgiver   ☐ Forgiving Redeemer   ☐ Truth Revealer

13

After some of Abraham's descendants (the Israelites) became slaves in Egypt, God called Moses to lead them out of Egypt and into Canaan, the land God earlier promised to Abraham.

Moses' Call to Leadership

Exodus 1:1-14; Exodus 3:1-17

a. God directed circumstances in Israel's family to place his son Joseph in Egypt as a prominent leader in order to prepare the way for Israel's family to follow.

b. Read Exodus 1:1-7. In what ways does verse 7 describe the growth of Israel's clan?

c. Read Exodus 1:8-14. What happened after a new Egyptian Pharaoh (king) came to power—one who did not remember Israel's son Joseph or the former Pharaoh's promises to Israel?

d. Read Exodus 3:1-10. What task did God have in mind for Moses? What special relationship to the Israelites did God claim?

e. Read Exodus 3:11-17. What was Moses supposed to tell the Israelites when they would ask him, "Who sent you?"
  • From God's instructions in verse 14?
  • From God's instructions in verse 15?

14

To free the Israelites, God sent a series of plagues upon Egypt, including the death of the firstborn in every family, but God protected those who appropriately expressed faith in Him.

The Plagues and Passover

Exodus 12:1-13, 21-23

a. To demonstrate His power over the false gods of Egypt and to convince Pharaoh to release the Israelites, God imposed a series of dreadful plagues upon Egypt. The final plague in that series involved the death of firstborn children and animals.

b. Read Exodus 12:1-13, 21-23.
  • What were the required characteristics of the animal to be sacrificed? See verse 5.
  • What were the Israelites supposed to do with the blood of this animal? See verses 7 and 22.
  • What sign would cause God to pass over a home without executing the plague of death? See verses 12-13, 23.
  • God established a memorial to remind the Israelites of this deliverance from death. What was this memorial to be called? See verse 27.

Put a mark beside each of the ways that Go

☐ Almighty Creator ☐ Supreme Authority ☐ Just Judge ☐ Merciful Protecto

☐ Holy God ☐ Faithful Promise Keeper ☐ Eternal Bein

15 Then Moses led the Israelites out of Egypt as God parted the waters of the Red Sea, preparing their way toward the promised land of Canaan.

Exodus of the Israelites from Egypt

Exodus 14:1-31

a. Read Exodus 14:1-12. What caused the Israelites' boldness (in verse 8) to be so quickly turned to fear (in verse 10)?

b. According to verses 1-2 & 9 in Exodus 14, what was the name of the place where the Israelites camped? Find the probable location of that place on the map on page 8.

c. Read Exodus 14:13-14. What expressions of faith in God do we see in the words of Moses?

d. As you read the remainder of the chapter, look for at least three major miraculous acts that God performed in order to make it possible for the Israelites to escape the Egyptians and to leave Egypt. Read Exodus 14:15-31. Identify and discuss the miracles that God performed.

16 In the wilderness between Egypt and Canaan, God, the perfectly Holy One, gave the Israelites a set of laws which express His hatred for what we know as *sin*.

The Ten Commandments

Exodus 20:1-17

a. God gave an extensive system of laws to the nation of Israel, but the core of that legal system was contained in what is often called the Ten Commandments. Read Exodus 20:1-17 and identify these ten foundational laws.

b. What do these laws reveal about the nature and character of God?

c. In your culture, which of these laws are often violated?

d. What do these laws reveal about the nature and character of mankind?

e. How many of God's laws would need to be broken for a person to be guilty of doing wrong—to have sinned? Think about Adam and Eve. See event 5 on page 14.

portrayed in the events on these pages:

☐ Universally Present Spirit ☐ All-Knowing One ☐ Relational Person ☐ Loving Father
☐ Authoritative Lawgiver ☐ Forgiving Redeemer ☐ Truth Revealer

17 God then directed Moses to build a portable place for worship where the Israelites could go to offer sacrifices and receive forgiveness of their sins.

Tabernacle in the Wilderness

Exodus 40:17-34; Leviticus 1:1-4, 10

Note: If this is a leader-guided study, the leader should be prepared to explain the functions and purposes of the major parts of the tabernacle. Download the Leader's Guide from the user support website for more information.

a. Read Exodus 40:17-34. Compare what you read here to the tabernacle drawing on page 10.

b. The tabernacle was a place of worship, but also a place where a person's sin could be atoned (covered or forgiven) by offering a sacrifice from his herds of cattle and goats, flock of sheep, or birds. The sacrificial animal would die as a substitute to atone for the person's sin. Read Leviticus 1:1-4 and 10-14. Summarize the procedure that was followed.

c. What similarities do you see between what was done here and what happened in event 8 on page 15 and event 14 on page 18?

18 On their way toward Canaan, the Israelites rebelled against God and were punished with deadly serpent bites, but God graciously provided a remedy for their afflictions.

Bronze Serpent

Numbers 21:4-9

a. Read Numbers 21:4-9 and identify each of the following parts of this story:
- Sin of unbelief and rebellion
- Judgment
- Confession
- Prayer for deliverance
- God's provision
- Faith
- Life

b. What did an Israelite have to do in order to be saved from death?

c. Keep this event in your mind because, later in the Bible's unfolding story, a very important teacher will refer back to it and will explain the prophetic significance of this event.

Put a mark beside each of the ways that God

☐ Almighty Creator   ☐ Supreme Authority   ☐ Just Judge   ☐ Merciful Protector
☐ Holy God   ☐ Faithful Promise Keeper   ☐ Eternal Being

19 After the Israelites entered Canaan, God ruled them through judges and kings, including King David whose kingdom God promised would endure forever through one special descendant.

Reign of King David

2 Samuel 7:1-16

a. Israel was ruled in Canaan by several judges, then later by a series of kings. David, the second king, was the greatest and godliest of them all. Read 2 Samuel 7:1-7. What kind of "house" did David want to build for God? Note: David gathered materials and made plans for a magnificent temple in Jerusalem, which was built later by his son, King Solomon.

b. Be aware that "house" sometimes also refers to a person's descendants or lineage. Read the last part of 2 Samuel 7:11 through verse

13. What kind of "house" did God promise to establish for David?

c. Read 2 Samuel 7:16. What indication do we have that this house-promise extends well beyond his son Solomon's reign?

d. Guess which Israelite tribe David was from. Hint: Remember Israel's promise to Judah in Genesis 49:10. See event 12 on page 17.

20 Throughout the history of the Israelites, God inspired His prophets to foretell many details concerning a special Israelite, a King and Savior, who would be born at some future time.

Prophecies of a Coming Messiah

Isaiah 7:14; 9:1-2, 6-7; 52:13—53:12

a. His birth: Read Isaiah 7:14. Recall that the promised conqueror of Satan was said to be the offspring of the woman, but no mention was made of a father. See event 7 on page 15. What possible connection do you see between Genesis 3:15 & Isaiah 7:14?

b. His birthplace: Read Micah 5:2. How does this verse relate to the scepter promise in Genesis 49:10? See event 12 on page 17.

c. His ministry in Galilee: Read Isaiah 9:1-2 & 6. Note that this area was near the Sea of Galilee.

d. His death: Read Isaiah 52:13—53:12. What bad things would be done to the man described here and what good things would result from his suffering?

e. His resurrection from death: Read Psalm 16:8-10. What does verse 10 indicate?

f. His eternal kingdom: Read Isaiah 9:6-7.

portrayed in the events on these pages:

□ Universally Present Spirit □ All-Knowing One □ Relational Person □ Loving Father
□ Authoritative Lawgiver □ Forgiving Redeemer □ Truth Revealer

21

21 At God's appointed time He sent His Son to Earth, born of a virgin named Mary, as the special King and Savior He had promised for centuries.

Birth of Jesus of Nazareth

Matthew 1:1-2, 18-25; Luke 2:1-14

a. Read the beginning of the genealogy of Jesus in Matthew 1:1-2. What special things do you remember about these ancestors of Jesus?

b. Read Matthew 1:18-25. What indications do we see here that Jesus was a unique child? Hints: the way He was conceived and His names "Jesus" and "Immanuel."

c. Read Luke 2:1-7 and compare to the prophecy of Micah 5:2. See event 20 on page 21.

d. Read Luke 2:8-14. Jesus was described as "a Savior, who is Christ the Lord." What do the words "Savior," "Christ," and "Lord" indicate? Hint: *Christ* is the Greek equivalent of the Hebrew word *Messiah* (one anointed to be king).

e. At the bottom of each of the double-page spreads on pages 22-31, place a mark beside each of the ways Jesus is portrayed in the four events on the two pages.

22 Before beginning His ministry, Jesus was personally tested by Satan but He resisted Satan's temptations with statements from God's Word in the Old Testament.

Temptations by Satan

Matthew 4:1-11

a. Jesus grew up in Nazareth where Joseph, His earthly father, worked as a carpenter.

b. At about age 30, Jesus was baptized by John the Baptist, a popular prophet of God, and was then led by God's Spirit into the wilderness where He was tempted by Satan.

c. Read Matthew 4:1-4. How would you summarize the nature of Jesus' first temptation? How did He respond?

d. Read Matthew 4:5-7. How would you summarize the nature of Jesus' second temptation? How did He respond?

e. Read Matthew 4:8-11. How would you summarize the nature of Jesus' third temptation? How did He respond?

f. How does Jesus' response to Satan's temptations differ from Eve's? See event 5 on page 14.

g. What words come to mind when you read how Jesus resisted Satan's temptations?

Put a mark beside each of the ways that Jes

☐ Humble Human Being ☐ Sinless Man ☐ Authoritative Teacher ☐ God in Human Fle

☐ Miracle Worker ☐ Rejected Messiah ☐ Israel's Promised King ☐ Willing Substit

23 God's prophet, John the Baptist, announced publicly that Jesus of Nazareth was the special King and Savior, God's Lamb, who would take away the sin of the world.

John the Baptist's Proclamation

John 1:29-34

a. After resisting Satan's grueling series of temptations, Jesus returned to the Jordan River where John the Baptist was baptizing repentant people and preaching about the coming Messiah. John called the crowd's attention to Jesus and made a remarkable proclamation.

b. Read John 1:29. Remember what we studied about sacrificial lambs taking away sins? See event 17 on page 20. What do you think John meant by this "Lamb of God" proclamation?

c. Remember the promise to Abraham in Genesis 12:3 and 22:18? See events 11 & 12 on page 17. Jesus was a descendant of Abraham. What is the connection between Jesus and the promise to Abraham?

d. Read John 1:30-34. What other special things do we learn about Jesus?

24 On one occasion, Jesus told a prominent religious leader that he needed to experience a spiritual birth in order to enter God's kingdom.

Encounter with a Religious Leader

John 3:1-18

a. Read John 3:1-4. How did Nicodemus interpret Jesus' statement about being "born again"?

b. Read John 3:5-8. What kind of rebirth was Jesus talking about?

c. What do you think Jesus meant when He talked about the need to be born again by the Spirit? Hint: Go back to John chapter 1 and read verses 10-13. "He" refers to Jesus.

d. Review the Israelites' experiences with the bronze serpent in Numbers 21:4-9. See event 18 on page 20. Now read John 3:14. Note: The title *Son of Man* is a common reference to Jesus. Based upon what we know about the Israelites' experiences, what do you think Jesus was predicting would happen to Him?

e. Read John 3:15-18. Summarize the main idea in these verses.

portrayed in the events on these pages:

Perfect Sacrifice ☐ Sin Forgiver ☐ Resurrected Savior ☐ Ascended Son of God
Satan Conqueror ☐ Worshipped Lamb of God ☐ Truth Revealer

25 On another occasion, Jesus explained to a woman from Samaria how God could permanently satisfy her spiritual thirst.

Encounter with a Samaritan Woman

John 4:3-42

a. In Jesus' day, people from Samaria were looked down upon and even hated by most Jewish people. Jews were forbidden by their religious leaders to even talk with them. They were considered to be religiously unclean. With that in mind, read John 4:3-9.

b. Read John 4:10-15. What kind of water was the woman thinking of and how did that differ from the "water" that Jesus was talking about?

c. Read John 4:16-18. What do we learn here about this woman's life?

d. Read John 4:19-26. What information about Himself did Jesus reveal to her?

e. Read John 4:28-29. How could Jesus know so much about this woman's life, since He had never met her before and was new to that area?

f. Read John 4:30, 39-42. How did other Samaritans respond to Jesus? What did they conclude?

26 Several times when Jesus declared that He was equal to and one with God, some people were greatly offended and attempted to kill Him.

Claims of Oneness with God

John 5:16-18; John 8:48-59; John 10:22-33

a. For a mere man to claim to be God or equal to God was one form of blasphemy. The penalty for blasphemy was death by stoning.

b. Read John 5:16-18. True or False? *By asserting that God was His Father, Jesus was acknowledging that He was of the same essential (and equal) nature as God.*

c. Read John 8:48-59. At the very beginning of our study, we learned that God is eternal—from everlasting to everlasting. What did Jesus reveal about Himself here? Read Exodus 3:14 and compare it with John 8:48-59. See event 13 on page 18.

d. Read John 10:22-33. Were the Jews accurate in their understanding—that Jesus was claiming to be God?

Put a mark beside each of the ways that Jes

☐ Humble Human Being ☐ Sinless Man ☐ Authoritative Teacher ☐ God in Human Fle
☐ Miracle Worker ☐ Rejected Messiah ☐ Israel's Promised King ☐ Willing Substitu

24

27 As He moved among the people, Jesus often lovingly but sternly warned them of the reality of eternal punishment in Hell and the urgent need to escape it.

Teachings about Hell

Mark 9:42-48; Luke 16:19-31

a. In an earlier lesson, we learned that an everlasting fire was created for the punishment of the Devil and his angels. See event 4 on page 13. Read Matthew 25:41. Jesus warned those who follow Satan that they too will experience that same eternal punishment.

b. Read Mark 9:42-48. What phrase did Jesus use in verse 48 to describe vividly what Hell is like?

c. Jesus once told about a man who died and went to Hell (Hades). Read Luke 16:19-31. According to what Jesus taught...

• True or False? *Hell is a place of conscious suffering.*

• True or False? *Once people are in Hell, they can escape.*

28 Out of compassion for hurting people and to demonstrate His divine power, Jesus healed the sick and disabled, cast out demons, and even raised people from the dead.

Miracles of Jesus

Matthew 4:23-24; John 11:1-45

a. Jesus performed many miracles to demonstrate that He was "the Son of God," as John the Baptist had said.

b. Read Matthew 4:23-24. What specific types of miracles did Jesus perform in this early ministry tour of the Galilee region?

c. Read John 11:1-4. What did Jesus say the ultimate purpose for Lazarus' sickness was?

d. Read John 11:5-16. What did Jesus know that His disciples did not know?

e. Read John 11:17-27. What did Jesus ask Martha regarding her belief in Him? What was Martha's response?

f. Read John 11:28-45 and look carefully at verses 40-45. In what positive way did many of the Jews, who witnessed this miracle, respond? Note: The *Jews* of the New Testament were basically the same people as the *Israelites* of the Old Testament.

portrayed in the events on these pages:

Perfect Sacrifice ☐ Sin Forgiver ☐ Resurrected Savior ☐ Ascended Son of God
Satan Conqueror ☐ Worshipped Lamb of God ☐ Truth Revealer

29 When Judas Iscariot (one of Jesus' twelve disciples) betrayed Him, Jesus did not supernaturally resist arrest but willingly submitted Himself to His captors.

Betrayal of Jesus

Matthew 26:1-2, 14-28, 45-56

a. Before you read from Matthew 26, read the prophecy in Psalm 41:7-9.

b. Read Matthew 26:1-2. What did Jesus know would happen to Him?

c. Read Matthew 26:14-28. Jesus was predicting that His body would be broken and His blood would be shed. How does Jesus' statement, in verse 28, clarify what John the Baptist said earlier, when he proclaimed, "Behold! The Lamb of God who takes away the sin of the world!"? See event 22 on page 22.

d. Read Matthew 26:45-56. Did Jesus have the power to resist arrest? Why do you think that He willingly submitted Himself to His captors?

30 Although Jesus was never proven guilty of any wrongdoing in any religious or civil court, He was unjustly flogged and condemned to die by Roman crucifixion.

Appearances before Unjust Judges

Matthew 27:1-2, 11-24

a. Read Matthew 27:1-2. What early indications do we see here that Jesus would not receive a fair trial?

b. Read Matthew 27:11-14. Did Jesus deny the accusation that He was the King of the Jews?

• In Genesis 49:10, God promised that the scepter, a sign of royalty, would not depart from the tribe of Judah. As a descendant of Judah, Jesus was qualified to be the King of the Jewish people. Review point d. in event 12 on page 17.

• Review points b., c., and d. in event 19 on page 21. As a descendant of King David, who was also from the tribe of Judah, Jesus was qualified to re-establish the royal reign of King David's family.

c. Read Matthew 27:15-24. What evidences do we see in this passage that Jesus was not guilty of the crimes for which He was being tried?

Put a mark beside each of the ways that Jes

☐ Humble Human Being ☐ Sinless Man ☐ Authoritative Teacher ☐ God in Human Fle
☐ Miracle Worker ☐ Rejected Messiah ☐ Israel's Promised King ☐ Willing Substitu

26

31 Jesus then died on a cross, as the perfect sacrificial Lamb for our sins and dealt the crushing blow to Satan that God had promised to Adam and Eve.

Crucifixion of Jesus

Luke 23:26-38; 1 Corinthians 5:7

a. The Jewish historian Josephus described crucifixion as "the most wretched of deaths." First, a prisoner was scourged mercilessly with a short, heavy whip. Then he was nailed to a cross where he suffered great shame and excruciating pain for hours before the rigors of crucifixion finally snuffed out his life.

b. Read Psalm 22:1-18. King David wrote this psalm about the Jewish Messiah approximately 1,000 years before Jesus was born and hundreds of years before crucifixion was used as a death penalty in Canaan. Look for indications that the man described here (the Messiah) would be dying by crucifixion.

c. Read Luke 23:26-38. What does Jesus' prayer in verse 34 tell us about Him?

d. Read the last phrase in 1 Corinthians 5:7 and think of the similarities between the Passover lambs that were killed in Egypt and Jesus' death on the cross. See event 14 on page 18.

32 As Jesus was dying, one guilty man who was being crucified beside Him placed his faith in Jesus and was granted the gift of life in a paradise beyond the grave.

A Repentant, Dying Thief

Luke 23:39-47

a. Read Luke 23:39-42. Which of these were true of the repentant criminal?
- ☐ He feared God.
- ☐ He acknowledged his own guilt.
- ☐ He acknowledged Jesus' innocence.
- ☐ He believed that Jesus was truly a king.
- ☐ He believed in life beyond death.
- ☐ He believed that Jesus could bestow some kind of kingdom favor on him.
- ☐ He made a simple faith-based request of Jesus.

b. Read Luke 23:43. Discuss the what, when, and certainty of Jesus' promise.

c. What other paradise did God provide much earlier in the Bible? See event 3 on page 13.

d. Read Luke 23:44-47. What did the Roman centurion conclude?

e. Read Mark 15:33-39. What other historical facts are given here regarding Jesus' death?

portrayed in the events on these pages:

Perfect Sacrifice ☐ Sin Forgiver ☐ Resurrected Savior ☐ Ascended Son of God

Satan Conqueror ☐ Worshipped Lamb of God ☐ Truth Revealer

33
On the third day after Jesus died and was buried, God supernaturally raised Him from the dead to demonstrate His power over sin, death, and Hell.

Resurrection of Jesus

Luke 24:1-12, 36-43

a. Read Hebrews 2:14-15. What purpose for Jesus' death do we see in verse 14? In verse 15?

b. Read Luke 24:1-12. Look for evidences that Jesus was no longer in the tomb.

c. Read Luke 24:36-43. What did Jesus do to prove that He was not just a spirit—that His physical body had been raised from the dead?

d. Because God raised Jesus from the dead...

• True or False? *We can have confidence that what Jesus said about Himself was true.*

• True or False? *We can have confidence*

that God was satisfied with Jesus' death as a payment for our sins.

e. As you think back over what we have studied, how would you answer this question: *Who is Jesus?* One great literary critic and philosopher has said that there are only three options:

☐ He was a lunatic. ☐ He was a liar.

☐ He was and is the Lord God just as He said.

34
After His resurrection, Jesus made numerous earthly appearances to His disciples and then ascended to Heaven to be with His Father.

Ascension of Jesus

1 Corinthians 15:3-8; Acts 1:6-11

a. Read 1 Corinthians 15:3-8. True or False? *More than 500 people saw Jesus alive after His resurrection and most of them were still living when this letter to the Corinthians was written.*

b. Read Acts 1:6-8. Acts 1:8 records the last words Jesus spoke on earth. Summarize the final statement that Jesus made to His followers.

c. Read Acts 1:9-11. What promise did the two men (angels) give to the followers of Jesus?

d. The next time Jesus appears in the story of the Bible is recorded a few chapters later. Read Acts 7:54-56. Where was Jesus at that time?

e. What is Jesus now doing in Heaven? Read Hebrews 7:24-25. Hint: The words "He" and "Him" (that appear in most versions of the Bible) refer to Jesus.

Put a mark beside each of the ways that Jes

☐ Humble Human Being ☐ Sinless Man ☐ Authoritative Teacher ☐ God in Human Fle

☐ Miracle Worker ☐ Rejected Messiah ☐ Israel's Promised King ☐ Willing Substitu

35 Soon after Jesus ascended, His disciples began to proclaim the good news about who Jesus was, what He did, and why people should trust in Him as their Savior.

Peter Proclaims the Good News

Acts 2:22-36

a. Ten days after Jesus ascended to Heaven, the Holy Spirit of God came upon the followers of Jesus, just as He had promised.

b. With the power of God's Spirit upon him, one of the disciples of Jesus (Simon Peter) presented his first message about Jesus. Based upon what he had personally seen and heard, what did Peter say about Jesus? Read Acts 2:22-26.

• His Life (verse 22)
• His Death (verse 23)
• His Resurrection (verses 24-32)

Note: Peter quoted Psalm 16:8-10 in verses 25-28. Be aware that this psalm was written by King David about 1,000 years before the earthly life of Jesus.

• His Ascension (verses 33-35)

c. What was Peter's overall conclusion regarding Jesus of Nazareth? Read verse 36.

36 Just as He promised during His earthly ministry, Jesus will return to take those who have truly believed in Him to be with Him in a heavenly paradise.

Jesus' Return for Believers

John 14:1-3; 1 Thessalonians 4:13-18

a. Beginning with this event, the final five events in this condensed version of the Big Story of the Bible have not yet occurred. To this point we have primarily been studying Bible history. But now we will see how seamlessly the Bible moves from Bible history (past events) into Bible prophecy (future events).

b. Before His death, what did Jesus tell his disciples in order to comfort them? Read John 14:1-3.

c. To learn more about this return of Jesus for believers, read 1 Thessalonians 4:13-18.

• What will happen to Jesus' followers who have already died?

• What will happen to Jesus' followers who are still alive when He returns?

d. Read 1 Corinthians 15:51-57. What additional information is given here regarding this return of Jesus Christ?

portrayed in the events on these pages:

Perfect Sacrifice ☐ Sin Forgiver ☐ Resurrected Savior ☐ Ascended Son of God
Satan Conqueror ☐ Worshipped Lamb of God ☐ Truth Revealer

37

Shortly after His return for believers, Jesus will come back with those He took to Heaven and will reign as King over the whole earth.

Jesus' Return as King

Revelation 19:11-19; Revelation 20:1-6

a. Be aware that the literary style of Revelation is highly symbolic. But as we look beneath the symbolic wording, four major facts emerge. Read Revelation 19:11-19.

• Jesus will return to the earth. (How do we know that this is the Jesus we have studied?)

• Jesus will be accompanied by the armies of heaven. (Who comprises these armies?)

• Jesus will defeat those who oppose Him at that time. (Who are these enemies of Jesus?)

• In doing this, God's wrath will be justly be- stowed. (Why is this judgment just and fair?)

b. Read Revelation 20:1-3. Who is the "old serpent" and what will happen to him? See events 4, 5, and 7 on pages 13-15.

c. Read Revelation 20:4-6. What will take place on the earth for 1,000 years? Where in our study have we seen predictors that Jesus will reign as a king?

38

Later, following a final attempt to lead a rebellion against God near the end of Jesus' earthly kingdom, Satan will be cast into the lake of fire that God prepared earlier for him.

Satan's Final Doom

Revelation 20:7-10

a. Prior to his eventual final doom, Satan will be bound for a period of 1,000 years. Read Revelation 20:1-3.

b. At the end of the 1,000 years, Satan will be released temporarily. What will Satan do at that time? Read Revelation 20:7-9.

c. Read and review Isaiah 14:15 and Matthew 25:41. See event 4 on page 13. Now read Revelation 20:10. What do we learn here about the nature of Satan's ultimate punishment?

d. Read and review Genesis 3:15. See event 7 on page 15. What is the connection between Genesis 3:15 (in the third chapter of the Bible) and the final doom of Satan described here (in the third chapter from the end of the Bible)?

Put a mark beside each of the ways that Jes

☐ Humble Human Being   ☐ Sinless Man   ☐ Authoritative Teacher   ☐ God in Human Fle

☐ Miracle Worker   ☐ Rejected Messiah   ☐ Israel's Promised King   ☐ Willing Substit

39

Then at the end of earthly time as we now know it, unbelievers will stand before God to be sentenced to eternal punishment for their sins.

Dreadful Destiny for Unbelievers

Revelation 20:11-15

a. As this event begins, what will happen to this present earth and heaven? Read Revelation 20:11 and compare it with 2 Peter 3:10.

b. Who do you think will be the Judge on this great white throne? Read Revelation 20:11-12a (first phrase of verse 12).

c. Books will play important roles when unbelievers stand before the Judge as He sits on this great white throne. Read Revelation 20:12-13.
  • What will be the role of the "the books"?
  • What will be the role of "the Book of Life"?

d. Read Revelation 20:14-15.
  Who will be cast into the lake of fire?
  • According to verse 14?
  • According to verse 15?

40

But God's story ends with wonderful news—everyone who has trusted Jesus as his or her Savior will enter a beautiful, sin-free paradise and live there eternally with God.

Blissful Destiny for Believers

Revelation 21:1—22:5

a. For believers to enjoy God's eternal paradise...
  ☐ They will go up to heaven for it, or...
  ☐ God will bring it down for them.
  Read Revelation 21:1-3 to find the answer.

b. Read Revelation 21:4-22:5 to learn more about this eternal paradise.
  • Who is "the Lamb"? Hint: See verse 14.
  • What will not be found in the new, holy city?
  • What are some of the most striking features of this new city?
  • Who will be allowed to live in this new para-dise? Read Revelation 21:27.

c. How long will they live there? Read Revelation 22:5.

d. Do you think that your name is written in the Lamb's Book of Life?
  ☐ Yes   ☐ No   ☐ Not sure
  Upon what do you base your conclusion?

ortrayed in the events on these pages:

Perfect Sacrifice ☐ Sin Forgiver ☐ Resurrected Savior ☐ Ascended Son of God
Satan Conqueror ☐ Worshipped Lamb of God ☐ Truth Revealer

GOD

What we have learned about our Creator:

1. The God of the Bible has always existed and will continue to exist forever. Because He is eternal, God referred to Himself as the "I AM" (Yahweh or Jehovah) which is translated in our Bibles as LORD.
2. By simply commanding it into existence, God created the world and everything in it. In its original condition, God's creation was perfect.
3. Throughout the Bible, this Creator-God continually demonstrated that He is all-powerful.
4. In contrast with false gods, the true God is perfectly holy (totally without sin).
5. As the Creator of mankind, God gave men and women clear commands to obey.
6. God is a righteous and fair Judge who must and will punish disobedience.
7. God loves us even when we disobey Him.

Which of these truths about God would you like to understand better?
Circle one or more numbers.

GOD   MAN   SIN   DEATH

SPIRITUAL DEATH

The Bible says: *But without faith it is impossible to please Him, for he who comes to God must believe that He is, and that He is a rewarder of those who diligently seek Him.* (Hebrews 11:6)

Our Faith Response: From the Bible we learn that one, and only one, true eternal and holy God exists, that He is our all-powerful Creator and just Judge, and that we are accountable to Him. Do you believe this?

MAN

What we have learned about mankind:

1. Human beings (people) are uniquely created by God, in His image. As such, we were given some qualities and abilities which God's other creatures did not receive.

2. These special qualities and abilities equip us to be caretakers of God's creation, a role that God has assigned to us.

3. God loves all human beings and desires that we be in perfect fellowship with Him and enjoy His presence.

4. Not only did God give us the responsibility and ability to obey Him, He also gave us the capacity to disobey.

5. Because God made us and owns us, every human being is accountable to Him.

6. Human beings were created with a material body as well as an immaterial spirit.

7. The spirit of man will never cease to exist; it will live forever in a resurrected body.

Which of these truths about mankind would you like to understand better?
Circle one or more numbers.

CHRIST   CROSS   FAITH   LIFE

ETERNAL LIFE

The Bible says: *And the LORD God formed man of the dust of the ground, and breathed into his nostrils the breath of life; and man became a living being.* (Genesis 2:7)

Our Faith Response: From the Bible we learn that we are made by God, loved by God, and that God deserves our full obedience. Do you believe this?

33

SIN

What we have learned about disobedience to God:

1. God created, loved, and provided for Adam and Eve but they rebelled against Him.
2. They disobeyed God, eating fruit from the one tree of which He told them not to eat.
3. Disobeying God is called *sin* and sin is a great offense to God, who is perfect and holy.
4. Adam and Eve's sin ruined the perfect relationship they had with God and with each other, resulting in a terrible physical and spiritual change for all mankind.

5. All mankind inherited their sinful, rebellious nature. Fighting, war, selfishness, and arrogance are all the results of the rebellion against God in our hearts.
6. The Bible says that we have all sinned. Everyone does things that he or she knows in his or her heart are wrong.
7. Because God is a holy and just judge, our sin cannot go unpunished.

Which of these truths about sin would you like to understand better?
Circle one or more numbers.

GOD MAN SIN DEATH

SPIRITUAL DEATH

The Bible says: *For all have sinned and fall short of the glory of God.* (Romans 3:23)

Our Faith Response: From the Bible we learn that we have sinned against God and deserve His righteous punishment. Do you believe this?

DEATH

What we have learned about the penalty for sin:

1. The essence of death is separation.
2. Adam and Eve died spiritually (became separated from God) the moment they sinned.
3. As their descendants, all human beings are born spiritually dead.
4. Physical death occurs when the human spirit separates from the body. Adam and Eve also experienced physical death, as do all of their descendants.
5. Physical death is not the end of our human existence. After a person dies, he or she will appear before God, who is the holy and just Judge of all mankind.
6. People who choose not to trust God's provision for sin and death will experience eternal death by being separated from God in everlasting conscious punishment.
7. Death, in all of its forms, is God's righteous judgment for sin.

Which of these truths about the penalty for sin would you like to understand better?
Circle one or more numbers.

CHRIST   CROSS   FAITH   LIFE

ETERNAL LIFE

The Bible says: *And as it is appointed for men to die once, but after this the judgment.* (Hebrews 9:27)

Our Faith Response: From the Bible we learn that we are facing God's judgment and cannot escape it on our own. Do you believe this?

CHRIST

What we have learned about Jesus Christ:

1. Soon after Adam and Eve sinned, God promised to send Someone who would conquer Satan.
2. Throughout the Old Testament, God gradually revealed who this person would be and that through His death forgiveness of sins would be provided for all who would trust Him.
3. To fulfill His promise, God sent His Son, Jesus, to rescue us from judgment.
4. God's Son was born of a virgin named Mary and was known as Jesus of Nazareth.
5. Jesus lived a completely perfect life of love and obedience to God.
6. During his earthly ministry, Jesus clearly and repeatedly demonstrated, through His claims and miracles, that He is God.
7. As both God and man in one perfect person, Jesus is truly unique and the only way to eternal life.

Which of these truths about Jesus Christ would you like to understand better?
Circle one or more numbers.

GOD   MAN   SIN   DEATH

SPIRITUAL DEATH

The Bible says: *Jesus said to him, 'I am the way, the truth, and the life. No one comes to the Father except through Me.'* (John 14:6)

Our Faith Response: From the Bible we learn that Jesus Christ is the perfect Son of God and the perfect Son of Man, the only way to eternal life. Do you believe this?

CROSS

What we have learned about the death and resurrection of Jesus Christ:

1. Because God is perfectly holy He must punish those who disobey His commandments.
2. Because God loves us even though we sin, He extends His mercy and grace to us in providing a just way in which we can be forgiven.
3. In the Old Testament, God established a sacrificial system through which sinners could have their sins forgiven.

4. Then God sent His Son Jesus to be the one perfect and final sacrifice for all sin.
5. Because religious and political leaders hated Jesus, they manipulated people and twisted the law to condemn Him to die.
6. Jesus willingly died in our place on a cross as our perfect sacrificial Lamb of God, the once-for-all payment for our sins.
7. Three days later, Jesus rose to life again, showing that God accepted Jesus' sacrifice as a just payment for our sins.

Which of these truths about the death of Jesus would you like to understand better?
Circle one or more numbers.

CHRIST   CROSS   FAITH   LIFE

ETERNAL LIFE

The Bible says: *Who Himself bore our sins in His own body on the tree, that we, having died to sins, might live for righteousness--by whose stripes you were healed.* (1 Peter 2:24)

Our Faith Response: From the Bible we learn that Jesus Christ, God's Son, died for our sins and rose from the dead to rescue us from death and give us eternal life. Do you believe this?

37

FAITH

What we have learned about trusting Jesus Christ:

1. In contrast to other religions of the world, the gospel of Jesus Christ offers eternal salvation in a manner that does not require people to work for it or earn it.
2. As sinful beings, no human being could earn salvation even if he or she wanted to and diligently tried to do so.
3. Through the death of His Son Jesus, our loving and righteous God provided the way to pay our sin debt.
4. Because Jesus paid the penalty for our sins, God extends salvation freely to us as a gift.
5. God promises to forgive us if we repent and believe (trust) in His Son, Jesus Christ.
6. Repentance occurs when our former false views of God, ourselves, and our sins are deeply changed to conform to God's view.
7. To believe is to trust Jesus (place our faith in Jesus), and Jesus alone, to save us.

Which of these truths about trusting Jesus Christ would you like to understand better?
Circle one or more numbers.

GOD   MAN   SIN   DEATH

SPIRITUAL DEATH

The Bible says: *For by grace you have been saved through faith, and that not of yourselves; it is the gift of God, not of works, lest anyone should boast.* (Ephesians 2:8-9)

Our Faith Response: From the Bible we learn that we must trust in Jesus' death on the cross as the only satisfactory payment for our sins, as we abandon our trust in other things that we formerly relied upon to save us. Do you believe this?

LIFE

What we have learned about eternal life:

1. When we repent and trust in Jesus, we pass from spiritual death to spiritual life.
2. The eternal spiritual life that God has promised becomes our present and everlasting possession, never to be forfeited.
3. Our spiritual life results in new desires and motivations, such as loving, obeying, worshipping, and serving God from our hearts.
4. Our new relationship with God frees us from the fear of death, knowing that our names are recorded in the Lamb's Book of Life and that death ushers us into God's presence.
5. It is now possible to experience the love, joy, and fulfillment that God desires for us.
6. We will enjoy life eternally in the presence of God in a beautiful, sinless, and pain-free paradise on a perfectly restored, new Earth.
7. Then and only then, will we understand the full significance of the Bible's story of hope.

Which of these truths about eternal life would you like to understand better?
Circle one or more numbers.

CHRIST   CROSS   FAITH   LIFE

ETERNAL LIFE

The Bible says: *Jesus said to her, 'I am the resurrection and the life. He who believes in Me, though he may die, he shall live. And whoever lives and believes in Me shall never die. Do you believe this?'* (John 11:25-26)

Our Faith Response: From the Bible we learn that Jesus alone has power over death and that He gives eternal life to those who trust solely in Him for the forgiveness of sins. Do you believe this?

A Personal Faith Response

Personalize the following words of Jesus. Instead of "the world," "whoever," and "he who," think of yourself as the object of Jesus' promises.

John 3:16-18

[16] For God so loved the world that He gave His only begotten Son, that whoever believes in Him should not perish but have everlasting life. [17] For God did not send His Son into the world to condemn the world, but that the world through Him might be saved. [18] He who believes in Him is not condemned; but he who does not believe is condemned already, because he has not believed in the name of the only begotten Son of God.

I now understand that the God of the Bible is the one True God. He is perfect and holy.

Through the teaching of the Bible I now see myself much differently than I previously did. I now realize that I was born with a sinful nature, that I have disobeyed God continually, and that my sin has deeply grieved God who made me and loves me. I know that my sin has separated me from God and that the just punishment for my sin is eternal separation from Him in a literal place of torment that the Bible calls *Hell*.

I understand that the death and resurrection of God's Son Jesus Christ is the only hope for me to be forgiven, for me to escape the eternal punishment for my sins, and for me to receive God's gift of eternal life.

I am now trusting Jesus Christ and His death on the cross, and no one or nothing else, as the only sufficient remedy for my sin problem and its dreadful consequences.

Basic Steps In Following Jesus

Begin Your Basic Steps as a Follower of Jesus Christ

USA: 1-877-959-2293
Canada: 1-877-690-1009
publish@abwe.org
www.GoodSoil.com

Lesson 1: The Story of Hope Review
Lesson 2: The ChronoBridge to Life Review
Lesson 3: Salvation Assurance & Security
Lesson 4: The Bible
Lesson 5: Prayer
Lesson 6: The Holy Spirit
Lesson 7: Personal Holiness
Lesson 8: Witnessing
Lesson 9: The Local Church
Lesson 10: God's Plan for You